The Mountain
We Climb

The Mountain We Climb

Dr. Wayne Swan

Prominent Books

Editing: Writer Services, LLC (WriterServices.net)
Cover Design & Book Layout: Writer Services, LLC

ISBN 10: 1-942389-21-3
ISBN 13: 978-1-942389-21-7

Prominent Books and the Prominent Books logo are Trademarks of Prominent Books, LLC

TABLE OF CONTENTS

Acknowledgments

This four-year effort is not about the power of one but the support of many. I learned so much in the process of writing *The Mountain We Climb*, and I could not have done it alone. In my case, it was friends, family, and well-wishers who stood behind the scenes helping me put my best effort forward. As a result, I had the pleasure of working with and learning from my coach, mentor and friend Robert Nahas of Writer Services, who believed in me and this project when others did not. I could not have achieved this goal without his sound and sage advice coupled with his shared passion for my success.

Special appreciation goes to photographers, mall studios, James Simmons, and Liana Hall for the book bio. To my family who climbed Kilimanjaro with me in spirit. To Francezia and Alana, who have always been in my corner giving of yourselves unselfishly!

In short, this book is about the power of successfully conquering your mountain and living in the transformation of that experience to face the what next. To encourage people around the globe to reach for and achieve success. No one knows more about this concept than my son Damien—my inspiration for writing this book. His never-give-up attitude is so contagious and is no doubt in my grandson Bently. To my daughter Damika for her inspiration and creative outlook on life.

And thank you also to John, my climbing partner, for your support and cheerleading every step of the way; and to the entire Climb Kili team, who aided us in successfully summiting Mount Kilimanjaro.

INTRODUCTION

In 2014, after more than a year of grueling physical and mental training, I successfully climbed and reached the summit of Mount Kilimanjaro. This was much more than a check on my bucket list; however, in the process, I gained experience and knowledge that completely transformed me. I came down the mountain a different man from the one who ascended.

Along the way, I found a correlation between facing life's struggles and challenges and those of climbing Kili. And I have certainly faced my share (and then some) of obstacles, from medical and identity crises to the death of a loved one, a failed business, two failed marriages and abandonment by friends. I know what it is like to have and to have not. I have had the best of times and the worst of times. I have experienced the feeling of victory and the agony of defeat.

In short, I am no different than anyone who has had start-and-stop moments in life. Unfortunately, most of us didn't grow up in perfect situations. Maybe we had great relationships but had bad parental guidance; the best education, but we made bad choices; found Mr. or Mrs. Just Right, only to realize that they were just All Wrong.

Everyone has experienced setbacks at one point or another, but for some, it seems like one thing after another blocks us from success. Then there are those who, when faced with obstacles, quit trying and refuse to set future goals. They say to themselves, *I cannot do this because I will not survive.* Or they say, *It's impossible. I know others can do it, but not me.* In doing so, they are talking themselves out of fulfilling their purpose and thereby never reaching the summit of their mountain.

We all can use motivation and inspiration, not only to set our goals but to achieve them. This book is for anyone who wishes to move past where they currently are. It's for those who feel they're losing more than they're winning. It's for those who want to figure out what really matters when it comes to being successful, happy and stronger. Everyone is both a student of life and a teacher ready to share what they've learned. And they must share it if we are to have a better world. That is my goal here; to share the wisdom I gained by doing something that started out to be a great idea but almost did me in. I want you to know how a regular guy made it past my lowest points of certain failure. Interestingly enough, whether climbing a mountain or overcoming a challenge in life, the rules and laws are the same.

Ultimately, this book is about how to find possibility when things seem impossible. And whether you believe there is a higher power or not, this book will give you the opportunity to look at this possibility in order to draw your own conclusion. It's safe to say that one has to at least entertain the idea that, since what you are doing so far has not worked out to your advantage, there is likely more that you need to know and discover for yourself. And who knows, maybe you will find God's promise for you, as well as the boundless strength that hides within each of us! In any case, you will be positively affected by this book if only by the many revelations of success and failure.

What if you could follow your dreams, and there were no obstacles out there that could stop you? This book is designed to help you develop an unstoppable mindset that can empower you to do just that.

You will be shown how to summon your inner strength and use this limitless power to overcome anything that comes your way. You will be both encouraged and inspired to live your life to the fullest, not just in spite of your challenges, but *because* of them.

Here are some things to consider before or while reading this book:

- Why am I not reaching my goals?

- What (or who) is stopping me from living a more purposeful life?

- What will it take for me to play "all in" without holding back?

- What will the benefits be to me and my family if I live a more determined and purposeful life?

- Have I honestly given myself every opportunity to win?

These thought-provoking questions are a good starting point that will inspire you to reflect on where you have been, where you are, and where you are going; it will also help you construct your plan for getting there.

This book will motivate you to take action, inspire you to be authentic and help you develop a victorious mindset. It will take you from a place of *I can't* to *I can* and equip you to overcome your challenges and fears today!

You will learn to align yourself with people who have succeeded where others have failed. You will also learn to ask each morning, "How will my mountain fear me today?" rather than you fearing the mountain.

CHAPTER ONE
What is the Goal?
(Identify the "What")

"If you don't know where you are going, then any road will take you there."

—Lewis Carroll

If someone asked you to describe your ideal life, what would you say? What if they asked you what your life's purpose is? If your response to either of these questions is "I don't know," then it's time to get serious about goal setting.

The truth is, everyone, no matter where they are in life, can benefit from goal setting. The process helps us identify the actions we must take in order to reach our objectives. Many don't realize, however, that it also helps us home in on what those objectives are. As Lewis Carroll so eloquently pointed out, journeying through life without direction will only get you lost. You need to be clear about your destination and go for it! Goals allow us to determine what our desired destination is and reach it. Moreover, the journey provides us with opportunities to grow and change in ways we may have never imagined. In short, setting goals and working toward them helps us to become better people.

How do we decide what goals we want to achieve? We start by examining our desires. Most of us have both short-term and long-term desires: we want to get an A in the class, find the right spouse, build a fulfilling career, and so on. That said, even as we dream about what the future may hold, we also have to live in the present and cope with circumstances in the here and now. We all have obstacles to overcome in order to reach our destination, and setting goals provides us with a visual road map to follow. Indeed, the more powerful we make our goals, the more we will strive to achieve them and ensure that they become reality.

Have you set goals and dreams for yourself? I don't just mean in terms of jobs or material objects, but the things that are truly important to you. Have you ever taken the time to sit down and write out what you most value and want to achieve during the course of your life? If you merely take some time to sit peacefully, go within and reflect, you will discover that there's much more to you and your dreams than you previously believed.

Take a moment to consider what really moves you and makes you excited for the future. If you had the ability to choose anything you want, be it a career or for recreation, what would it be? What do you want to be remembered for, and what are you so passionate about that you feel like you simply have to try it? What event or milestone would you be thrilled to reach? Once you're able to provide answers to those questions, you'll feel much more confident in your ability to handle the future.

One of the most critical steps you can take is to write down dreams—doesn't matter whether you're having them while awake or asleep. This may seem silly at first, but don't dismiss it. Let your wildest dreams take root without editing them based on what you think is possible or probable. Then and only then, allow yourself to prioritize their importance. In this way, we can move from the abstract of fantasy and start turning those dreams into a reality. The goal here is to move from *dreaming* to *action*. There are several ways to do this:

- Be realistic. Remember that being realistic starts with being "real." Creating something tangible is possible, but not if you start off with dreams that are outlandish and beyond the scope of reality. At the same time, don't sell yourself short. You have more potential than you might think, so even goals that seem far off, such as a dream job, may be possible to obtain by taking small but focused steps.

- Be Specific. One reason that our dreams don't become tangible is because we never conceptualize them fully. Resist the urge to be lazy or wishy-washy—when setting out ambitions for your future, be clear and concise.

- Achievability: This is different than making dreams realistic. Achievability gives you something specific to strive for. While you want to start out with dreams that can become reality, you also want to create an endpoint in mind.

- Measurability: While you're on the path to attaining your goals, try to set up a series of intermediate goals or milestones along the way so that you can ascertain whether you're on track.

- Time Frame: Attaching a time frame to a set of goals ensures that you won't get too far off track when trying to reach them. When creating a list of specific goals, give yourself a time frame to accomplish each one; this will motivate you to work harder.

- Be Accountable. While you shouldn't punish yourself for not reaching your goals when you're really trying, you should, however, hold yourself accountable for slacking off. A good way to do this is to tie your goals to some other marker (i.e. a person). This makes you responsible to others as well as yourself. For example, if your goal is to have a house with a big yard, you might envision your children playing there. Your desire to get this for them will keep you honest and on track.

As mentioned earlier, there are short-term goals and long-term goals, and while the two are often linked, there are also some important differences.

A short-term goal is something an individual strives to accomplish in the near future, which can mean today, a month from now or within the year. Regardless of the exact time frame, it's something that you want to reach for relatively soon. Short-term goals are also useful because they are often steps one takes to reach more important, longer-term goals. As Barbara Walters said, "One may walk over the highest mountain one step at a time."

Here are some examples of short-term goals:

- Landscape my front or backyard.

- Paint the interior or exterior of my home.

- Clean out my basement or attic.

A long-term goal is, obviously, a goal that one keeps in mind for further down the road. It will usually take more than twelve months to achieve and require a good deal of time, foresight and planning. One constructs long-term goals by taking a long, hard look at one's dreams and desires and deciding what they want to have or be doing in, say, five or ten years. Again, achieving short-term goals should be part of the process in achieving your long-term success.

Here are some examples of long-term goals:

- Get a law or doctorate degree.

- Start my own business.

- Plan and save for retirement.

Tips When Setting Long-Term Goals:

- Start from the distant future and work your way back. For example, look all the way to retirement age for your ultimate goals, then visualize the steps you took to get there.

- Set time-spaced goals. Where do you want to be in five years? Ten? Twenty?

- In setting these time-spaced goals, what are some steps you think you should be taking at each point in order to achieve your ultimate dream?

- Write everything down to ensure that you're making some measurable achievements every single month.

- When you start hitting goals, look back and determine whether your path needs to be adjusted. Are you hitting goals faster than you anticipated? Slower? Tweak as needed.

Prioritization of Goals

Deciding what to do first and adjusting accordingly is called **prioritizing**. In order to prioritize, you need to decide what's most important to you at the moment. This will help you set goals that you can start working on immediately. Some tips for prioritization include:

1. Pick what's most important to you right now.

2. Make this goal the focus of your attention.

3. As you get on the right path to achieving this important goal, add other priorities as you think you can manage them.

4. Be flexible. Life changes, so prepare yourself to change focus and reprioritize as needed.

In June of 2013, my goal was to successfully reach the summit of Mt. Kilimanjaro in February 2014.

Chapter Two

"Vision is the spectacular that inspires us to carry out the mundane."

—Chris Widener, author of *The Art of Influence*

Vision is defined as something that you can imagine, or a picture that you can frame within your mind.

Every achievement starts out in the heart and brain; anyone who has ever achieved anything first envisioned themselves doing it. Take athletes, for example. Regardless of their chosen sport, they often say they visualized their objective before the event—the golfer sees the ball falling into the hole on the first stroke, hockey players see the puck flying into the net. They envision the achievement within their mind then act it out in real time.

For regular people, setting a vision is just as important. Every day while preparing to climb Mt. Kilimanjaro, or "Kili," I saw myself standing on Uhuru Peak. During my training sessions, I acted out my vision by slowly jogging with a thirty-pound pack on my back. Those around me may have thought I looked like a fool, but I didn't allow it to affect me. My odd behavior had a purpose—it was part of a larger vision—and in acting out this vision, I was preparing myself for the actual journey. While reaching for your goals, you too will appear strange and perhaps foolish, but keep going!

No matter how adept you are at visualization, there will be obstacles you cannot foresee. That's life. The important thing is to not get discouraged; just be ready to expect the unexpected. When you encounter something that seems impossible to overcome, like a smooth rock face, just picture yourself at the top of your goal, and you'll be better able to conquer the obstacle in front of you. Keep dreaming big and believe that you can make your dreams possible for yourself and those around you. Have faith in your ability to accomplish the seemingly impossible, and dare to believe even when others do not.

"Now faith is the substance of things hoped for, the evidence of things not seen."

—Hebrews 11:1

When I told them what I planned to do (climb Mt. Kilimanjaro), friends and family tried to talk me out of it. *You are crazy! You could get injured or die,* they said. *You are not a professional climber, you know.* I couldn't argue with that; I had never even been exposed to high-altitude conditions. Yet I continued to believe that I could accomplish my goal.

Throughout your life, you will encounter people who

don't believe you can accomplish the things you set out to do. The best thing to remember in these situations is to keep the faith and know that as long as you're following a concrete plan, your goals and dreams are obtainable and realistic. Your dream or goal is probably not the same as those who doubt you, and if you've done the preliminary goal-setting work (i.e. listing your desires and prioritizing them), you're better equipped than them to know that it's possible.

Maintaining a levelheaded perspective is critical when pursuing a long-term goal, especially if it's a dream you've held for a long time or is your top priority.

What I am actually speaking of here is *purpose*. Purpose is the objective we were put on this planet to accomplish. It's the talent that we are imbued with, the gift we can best express uniquely and individually. Talents or gifts are inextricably linked with purpose, and yet pursuing such goals can still be overwhelming. Ask yourself, "What is one of my greatest talents, and how can I incorporate it into something I do regularly?" Then try making that the focus of your goals and dreams.

Your purpose may seem unrealistic to you. Yet by incorporating it into your vision, you can start to make it tangible. Have you ever been uncertain about what you want to achieve and still been successful? If you have, great! Just recognize that this is not a common phenomenon. In order to achieve your vision, it is important to be certain of what your purpose is; that way, you can concretely lay out a plan to reach it.

A note of caution: if you take a path other than the one

that leads toward your ultimate goal, you will deny yourself any chance of success. You will also quite possibly fall short of your life's purpose and potential and forfeit the chance to be happy as well.

A vision gives you an entirely new meaning and perspective that will assist you in striving to reach your ultimate goal and potential. You suddenly see your purpose as a puzzle, with short-term goals as the pieces that lock together and fit to make a greater whole. Each piece is not a chore but an exciting new challenge to solve on the way to your ultimate goal. Picture your own future in your head and see yourself reaching your potential. This may seem like wishful or idle thinking, but I can assure you, it is not. Whereas wishful thinking means imagining something that is highly unlikely and possibly flies in the face of logic, *purposefully* thinking of a specific future with a clear head is a powerful exercise by which you clarify your *intent*. At first, this may seem difficult, but it's an important step of a process that involves resetting your mind in order to make the impossible concrete. In clearly seeing your future, that future becomes part of the present.

Dare to imagine. A common trick people use in order to lose weight is to picture themselves as having already reached their "target." By picturing yourself at the goal weight and imagining how you feel at that weight, you are daring yourself to believe. This can work with anything. Imagine sitting in your dream car and feeling the leather against your skin, your hand on the powerful gear-shift.

Again, this may seem like idle fantasy, but when you

imagine yourself as already having what you desire, and use your senses to engage with it, your desired goal becomes more tangible. As it says in the Bible: "Faith is the substance of the things hoped for, and the evidence of things not yet seen." Faith is necessary to believe you can achieve your goals, but faith without works is not faith at all. In order to back up this faith, you must create a plan that puts your faith into action.

As with anything else, when visualizing your end result, practice makes perfect. While pursuing my goal, I practiced both physically and mentally. In addition to training my body, I watched videos and read material from those who had already scaled Kilimanjaro, successfully and unsuccessfully, as this would give me a greater sense of realism. I also continued to picture myself at the top; this way I was aware of the possibility of failure but framed my journey from a successful standpoint. I saw myself in the future. See yourself in the future—NOW! What does it look like?

That said, it's important to balance your vision with real-world planning and analysis. For example, cost must be taken into account. Everyone who sets out on a major project, be it construction or a sporting event, does so after figuring out the cost and/or creating a budget. This allows us to keep our goals within the realm of reality. In fact, in some cases, painting a realistic financial picture can be just as important as determination, preparation and training.

It has been said that a journey of a thousand miles begins with a single step. Your ultimate goal will be achieved by scoring several small-scale victories, and being straightforward about these steps will allow you to take the guesswork out of the equation and help you move toward the goal itself.

When visualizing the realization of any goal, remember to be as detailed as possible. Ask questions of yourself and of authorities (those who have already achieved what you're setting out to do or, if your goal is original, a comparable example). By seeking out advice and guidance, you'll stay motivated and grounded and avoid heartache and wasted time.

Sometimes, we can draw motivation from those who **haven't done** what we're trying to do. I remember my father saying, "I have been where you are, but you have never been where I am." He was letting me know that though we were different, and though he supported my path, my goals and my aspirations, he also had wisdom born of life experience.

Once you're clear about what your goal is, commit to it fully by taking steps toward it each and every day. One day, you may only be able to take a very small step, while other days will feel like you've reached a milestone of an exciting adventure. Set a goal, then share it with family and friends; this will help you to remain motivated and keep you accountable. By doing all this, you've created a road map to your goal.

It's important to frequently evaluate your progress and review your goals as this will also show you where you need to tweak and adjust. Reaching the "summit" takes time, so try to enjoy the hike while you travel, and celebrate each milestone—large and small—that you achieve along the way.

Now let's start climbing!

Once I had chosen the path above, climbing is exactly what I started to do. For while much of my careful preparation involved screening videos, reading articles and talking to a friend, *moving* is what brought my vision to life. I had a clear vision in my head of my goal, and I became inspired to achieve the impossible; I became someone who imagined.

As I did this, I noticed my mindset changing. To be honest, I wasn't entirely sure when I began to believe that I'd actually be able to do it. My task certainly was daunting. Yet, slowly through my self-visualization, I began to realize I had gained a new perspective, not only with regard to this goal but to life in general. That's the thing about positive thinking—it affects everything! You will begin to achieve more goals than you thought you were capable of; you can also become a better spouse, sibling, business partner, friend, parent and more. John C. Maxwell wrote: "If you are willing to change your thinking, you can change your feelings. If you can change your feelings, you can change your actions. And changing your actions based on good thinking can change your life."

It has been said many times that "doing the same thing again and again, expecting a different result is the meaning of insanity." I've learned that one of the main reasons people don't end up realizing their goals is because they continue to desire the same thing without changing their thinking. Doing the same thing over and over again may not be as terrible as one may believe, as long as that repetition results in concrete steps of achievement or visualization.

"Nurture great thought, for you will never go higher than your thoughts."

—Benjamin Disraeli

If you really want to make progress in achieving a goal or project, you must begin to take action. Yet the success of taking that action relies in great measure on the thinking you've adopted beforehand. The brain must be prepared to undertake a task before the hands begin moving to complete it.

CHAPTER THREE
The Plan

"You're off to great places! Today is your day! Your mountain is waiting, so... get on your way!"

—Dr. Seuss

Do you enjoy making plans? The Business Dictionary defines a plan as a "written account of intended future course of action (scheme) aimed at achieving specific goal(s) or objective(s) within a specific timeframe. It explains in detail what needs to be done, when, how, and by whom, and often includes best-case, expected-case, and worst-case scenarios."

I personally love planning, especially when it comes to travel and adventures. If I'm traveling overseas, I research the country and city I'll be visiting, including national and local laws, public transportation, a list of things I'd like to do and places where I'd like to eat. I carefully choose my hotels and find out the best places to rent a car and how much I should pay for a taxi.

This may seem very "type-A" to some, but this extensive planning has always benefitted me and my family. It's saved me time, money and heartache and made my journey more pleasurable. This same approach, I believe, can be applied to virtually every facet of a person's life.

"It has been said that out of all the things men are able to recycle, Time is not one of them."

—Author Unknown

It may be hard to believe, but the average person spends more time planning a singular event or vacation than they do mapping out their goals.

They don't realize that if you don't plan ahead, dreams, goals and, eventually, life will fall by the wayside. Not only will you miss opportunities, a lack of planning can come back to haunt you in the form of financial penalties. Sure, we all "wing it" from time to time, but it certainly isn't a philosophy to live by if one wants to achieve his or her ultimate goals and desires. As Benjamin Franklin said, "When you fail to plan, you plan to fail."

Once you have identified your dreams and goals, the next step is to create a plan for each and every one of them. Success appears magically only for the lucky few, and those people almost always have significant help along the way. For the rest of us, planning is an essential ingredient for success.

Take some time to consider why putting forth a plan for your life is so important:

1. A plan is what gives a person direction, allowing them to realize where they are trying to go and how they are going to get there. Without one, there is no focus, much less direction, and an individual risks wasting time and failing to do things that create tangible benefit for the future.

2. Tangibility also relates to the requirements of realism and actuality, which I mentioned in the chapter on goal-setting. If your personal dreams have felt, well, like **dreams**, it doesn't necessarily mean they are unrealistic; in fact, it is more likely you don't have a plan in place to achieve them. A plan lays out action steps, guiding you to place one foot in front of the other and make the impossible possible.

3. When you leave things to chance, you give away your power. You may find yourself at the mercy of others to deal with even the smallest unforeseen events, and life feels like an uncontrollable ride. However, a plan puts you back in the driver's seat and gives you a measure of control.

4. A plan takes away stress and provides peace. In fact, the mere act of creating a plan and knowing it is in place reminds you that you have a higher purpose for which you are now living. Even when you are having a down day, you will view it from a different perspective. Rather than getting lost in despair, anger and confusion, you will remember that there is a larger goal for which you are striving.

5. A purpose-driven life is a life worth living. By choosing to live "on purpose," you are embracing the idea that there is a greater plan in mind—not just your plan for yourself, but perhaps an even higher calling. You no longer have to stumble around just to continue to exist. By embracing purpose, you now have something to grasp onto, a mast to guide you through even the most perilous storms.

6. A plan provides not only purpose but passion as well. Reaching success after laying out a careful plan can give you a true rush. You know you are on a journey, and as you climb each rung, you will get more enjoyment out of both the present and the future.

7. A plan is also empowering. No longer are you beholden to an amorphous outside force but to YOUR own purpose. Yes, you still have to go to your job and honor other commitments. Yet you realize that ultimately you are your own boss and have the ability and power to live your life the way you want to.

8. A plan not only honors you but a higher cause. In laying out your plan, you are acknowledging that He has placed you here with a purpose and demonstrating your willingness to be a steward of the gifts He has given you.

9. A plan enlivens your subconscious mind and gives it something to work toward. You know that nagging feeling you get in the back of your mind sometimes? That's your subconscious reminding you that you have a purpose to fulfill. Instead of nagging, wouldn't it be better if your subconscious was rejoicing that you are on a path to realizing your life's goals?

10. Freedom. It is what everyone on this planet desires. While we may live in a "free" country, we are beholden to forces greater than ourselves. By planning our lives, we take back some of the personal autonomy that is our birthright. By shaping our own destiny, we are able to experience true freedom.

Nothing in my life required more planning than Mt. Kilimanjaro. To prepare, I had to embark on a very challenging training program so that I would be physically and mentally prepared before I ever placed a foot on the mountain. For example, Bermuda, where I live, is at an elevation near sea level, compared to Kilimanjaro's elevation of 19,341 feet or 5895 meters from sea level. That meant my training program would have to include preparation for a significantly higher altitude, and its effects, from Day 1. Taking into account my age, my maximum heart rate should be 170, which meant my target heart rate while exercising should be between 111 and 145.

While my ultimate goal was to climb Mt. Kilimanjaro, a smaller, ancillary goal would be to increase my overall stamina and fitness. It would not only improve my physical ability but increase my mental confidence—a necessary combination for taking on this kind of challenge. This vastly increases your enjoyment of the activity as well as adding to your overall sense of achievement. Many have reached the "Rooftop of Africa," as Kili is often called, but that doesn't mean it is a simple hike. Committing to a solid fitness program can determine whether or not you reach the summit.

Preparation

Meticulous planning isn't an accident; it **prevents** accidents. It is also a way to demonstrate to yourself that you are "all in."

Lay out what you need to do well in advance. When I decided to climb Mt. Kilimanjaro, I gave myself six months to get myself in the best physical and mental shape of my life. That means I had to start the planning process well before that. The same is true of any goal—even if you don't need to begin taking action immediately, it's best to work out a specific timeline from the beginning of the project to completion. Otherwise, you may not have the time and resources needed to achieve your ultimate goal.

Being Equipped

There is a saying: "Today's preparation determines tomorrow's achievements."

A critical part of the planning process is to make sure you have all the tools needed to achieve your goal. Obtaining these tools is another incremental or short-term goal that will increase your readiness and anticipation for the larger achievement. I had an extensive list of gear I needed for Mt. Kilimanjaro, and when I obtained it, I knew that the final tangible step before leaving was complete. The same is true if, for example, your long-term goal is to have your own company. You must obtain the equipment to build the infrastructure and create, sell and distribute your product; your list of equipment might even include employees and proper attire—whatever you need to make your dream a reality. Make sure you run figures and tables as well so that you can answer questions immediately if and when you are asked, say, for example, while applying for a loan. As your goal continues to take shape in your mind, ask yourself whether you have the proper tools, information and resources to successfully reach your summit.

Remember, *"Success occurs when opportunity meets preparation."*

—Zig Ziglar

Former United States Senator Mark Udall said it best:

"You don't climb mountains without a team, you don't climb mountains without being fit, you don't climb mountains without being prepared, and you don't climb mountains without balancing the risk and rewards. And you never climb a mountain on accident—it has to be intentional."

CHAPTER FOUR
Overcoming Obstacles

"Wanting something is not enough. You must hunger for it. Your motivation must be so absolutely compelling in order to overcome the obstacles that will invariably come your way."

—Les Brown

In life, the road is not always smoothly paved; in fact, there will always be unforeseen potholes and roadblocks that blindside you, no matter how well you've planned things out. When a person achieves his or her goals, it is not because they did not face challenges but because of the choices they made in order to deal with them.

As Booker T. Washington said, "Success is to be measured not so much by the position that one has reached in life as by the obstacles which he has overcome."

When faced with inevitable obstacles placed in your path, what will you do? Where and to whom will you turn for help? When you come to a crossroads, will you choose decisively whether to go right or left? Or, will you go back from whence you came and look for another path?

These are some of the many questions I faced when scaling Mt. Kilimanjaro, and as I got closer to my dream, I learned more and more that the answers you learn when striving for your greatest goal are the answers that will stick with you the rest of your life.

Facing Mountains

By now, you know that working toward a goal is like climbing a mountain, whether literal, as in my case, or figurative. Sometimes, we get so caught up in the enormity of our goal, we forget that every journey, no matter how long or arduous, begins with a single step. For me, that step was not taken at the foot of the mountain but months earlier when I began that rigorous training program. Your first step may be going back to school or learning a trade so you can begin a new career or start a business of your own. The key is to stop procrastinating, push past your fear, and start moving in the direction of your goal.

When facing any mountain, the peak is the goal, but the journey is the challenge and, in many ways, what makes reaching the peak so fulfilling. There will be times when the path seems uphill in every direction; you may even have moments when you doubt whether the goal is worth the trouble.

Other times, you will be working "all systems go" when suddenly you're hit with trials that challenge your core beliefs in yourself. However, even these darkest moments have a divine purpose. As President Richard Nixon once said, "Only if you have been in the deepest valley can you ever know how magnificent it is to be on the highest mountain."

Of this I speak from experience. Early one morning in February 2008, I received the call every parent dreads. Damien, my only son, twenty-two years old, had been involved in a terrible traffic accident, and I needed to get to the hospital as soon as possible because it did not look good. As I raced to the emergency room, my mind raced with horrific scenarios of what I would find when I got there. I thought about all the plans Damien and I had made together, all the projects we would complete side by side.

"This is my son! I should not be burying him; he should be burying me!" I shouted this, even as I tried to remain positive in the face of what appeared to be certain calamity.

Finally, I pulled into the car park at the hospital's emergency entrance, but before exiting my vehicle, I took a moment to turn inward to my faith. I prayed to the Lord to give me His peace and wisdom so that I may be strong for my son, his mother and sister, and the rest of the family.

Inside the hospital, the anxiety was almost unbearable as we waited for a post-surgical meeting with the doctors. I spent my time comforting family and friends who had assembled to pray for Damien's welfare, but truthfully, it helped me to have a distraction. Finally, the doctors came out to speak with us. They were not too optimistic.

Damien had sustained a severe head injury, and they were doing what they could to relieve pressure on the brain while he remained in a coma in the Intensive Care Unit. Now all we could do was wait to see how his body would react. What a mountain to face!

When we are confronted with such experiences, we often wish that we weren't present or had done something differently to avoid the circumstances we find ourselves in. As in my case, there was nothing I could have done to prevent Damien's accident. Yet wishful thinking does not give us insight. Instead, we must ask ourselves what we can do to learn and grow from the situation. Struggles, challenges and obstacles are placed in our paths to stretch the muscles of our character, and while they can be deeply disheartening, they are important ingredients for the dynamic growth of self. These circumstances bring to the surface qualities that we were not aware we even possessed—qualities which often come to shape greatness and define our purpose as human beings.

Note: there are many different kinds of life obstacles (mountains). These are the things that seem to hold you back or block your path to achieving your goals. They come in all different shapes and sizes, but understanding the kind of "mountain" you face will help you learn how to overcome it. "Attitude determines altitude," as climbers like to say. Your attitude is the key.

Here are some of the different types of mountains you may face in life:

- Challenges: They help you develop your character and add to your experience.

- Hurdles: You must have momentum in your life in order to leap over them.

- Potholes: These cause you to slow down and use caution when taking your next step.

- Walls: They force you to look for a ladder you can climb.

- Fear: It's what keeps you frozen and indecisive. You must find a way to shift it so you can move.

- Mountains: These are the tallest of obstacles, and you must take the time to find ways around them.

  - External mountains: These are forces outside of your control, such as the economy, natural disasters, physical handicaps and political strife.

  - Internal mountains: These are personal issues that you have (or can gain) control over, such as your time, finances and talents.

- Yourself: Sometimes we get in our own way and can be the biggest obstacle of all. We conquer this by releasing limiting beliefs and changing our behavior.

Once a person understands what is holding them back, they can begin to take action that puts them back on the right path. An important piece here is the realization that, when seen from the right perspective, the "mountains" in our life can help us develop our identity and purpose.

To overcome mountains with regard to your business, relationships or identity:

Be honest with yourself. If you ignore or fail to acknowledge the mountains in your path, it will be difficult for you to overcome them and reach the "summit", whatever that may be for you. You will begin to blame everything and everyone else, rather than resolving your issues or habits that you subconsciously use to self-sabotage. In my case, there never seemed to be enough time to do what I needed to do. Eventually, I came to realize that it was not a lack of time but my own poor management of the time I had that was keeping me from my goals. I needed to have a heart-to-heart with the man in the mirror in order to steady myself and get back on track.

Learn from external mountains. While exceedingly frustrating, obstacles beyond your control have much to teach you. They require you to learn patience, and the more difficult the mountain or obstacle, the more patience will be required to overcome it. Remain focused on your goal while waiting for the smoke to clear and things to settle down.

This helped me while slowly trekking from one campsite to the next in Africa. We had started our journey in good weather and spirits, but one hour into our hike, rain, mist and fog had reduced both our visibility and our pace to what felt like a snail's crawl. Even though I could only see two feet in front of me, I knew that I had to be patient and trust our guide while staying on the path. We had no control over the weather, but our plan called for us to keep moving forward while waiting for conditions to improve. When that eventually happened, we looked back and were shocked to see how much ground we had covered! Once I realized the progress we had made during this difficult time, it gave me the fire and energy to press forward with renewed determination. During this seemingly useless "downtime", we had in fact been building the momentum required to reach our goal!

Discipline yourself to remain focused. In today's world, we are so accustomed to being busy that it is very easy to become distracted with mundane tasks. Over time, I learned that true discipline means placing your focus on what will benefit you and get you closer to your goals, no matter what is happening externally. I came to the realization that I had to take responsibility for my own actions. I identified and removed every distraction in order to stay on track, slowly but steadily progressing forward.

Use your imagination. Whenever possible, I use creative visualization to overcome obstacles. As I mentioned earlier, I thoroughly planned my trip to Africa and the steps I would need to take while there in order to achieve my goal. This included daily intensive physical and mental training so as to give myself every chance to reach the summit of Kilimanjaro. There would still be significant challenges, and I came up with creative ways to overcome them. For example, for a laugh on a hot day, I would dress in my hiking gear (minus my heavy winter coat, gloves and balaclava; after all, I live in Bermuda!), strap my thirty-pound rucksack to my back, and walk on the main roads, which are very hilly and take me past the lush shorelines and beaches. While this was part of my rigorous training program, I also enjoyed watching the bewildered reactions of passersby. I know to them I looked crazy and out of place, but that was all part of the fun. I did this three or four times a week, varying my direction, distance and pace, and imagining my success with every step! Take the time to lay out a plan, and once you have one, find ways to make your way through it that are fun and engaging but also present you with the opportunity to overcome potential challenges.

CHAPTER FIVE
Perspective

"It is not the mountain we conquer, but ourselves."

—Edmund Hillary

"Never measure the height of a mountain until you have reached the top. Then you will see how low it was."

—Dag Hammarskjold

Success is no accident. Sure, there have been instances where someone gets "lucky" and/or stumbles upon a great idea or financial windfall, but the vast majority of us must devise a plan and commit to it by putting one foot in front of the other. Here are a few points that will help you reach your dreams and goals:

1. Remember that you are responsible for your success. In times of distress, you should be prepared to rescue yourself. No one else is the cause of your success, so no one else should be blamed for you failing to reach your goals. Take full responsibility for your actions.

2. Optimism is key. Envisioning success and holding that image in your mind helps make it a reality. Try to remain positive because positive thoughts will overcome negative ones and allow you to press forward towards eventual success.

3. A healthy level of self-esteem is paramount for success. If you've struggled with low self-esteem, seek whatever help you need to change it. This could be reading inspiring books, praying and meditating, and celebrating things you have already accomplished. Do not waste time dwelling on past mistakes, but instead recognize the lessons you've learned from them and move on.

4. Recognize that you are here in this world on purpose and for a purpose. And, who knows? It has been said by many that God's plan is, and always has been, for us to live fulfilling and abundant lives. But that's for you to self discover.

5. Your success is found in your pursuit of personal passions. As Mark Twain said, "Find a job you love doing and you will never have to work a day in your life." Of course, this does not apply only to work, but to any goal you want to achieve. As English actor Andrew Garfield said, "I've realized that at the top of the mountain, there's another mountain." In other words, there's always another goal to set your sights on and achieve!

6. Surround yourself with successful people and emulate the methods by which they set goals and motivate themselves to achieve them. Why reinvent the wheel?

7. Avoid negative people. They are toxic and will be a hindrance to your success.

Remember that there will be times when you will experience failure (whether actual failure or the fear of it), self-doubt and indecision. Your success will hinge upon your ability to overcome these emotional obstacles by way of channeling intellectual and action-based positivity. Revisit your plans and breathe deeply as you envision them coming into fruition. Try to feel into your success as if it has already happened.

The Story of the Butterfly

A man found the cocoon of a butterfly. One day, a small opening in the cocoon appeared. He sat and watched the emerging butterfly for several hours as it struggled to squeeze its body through the tiny hole. Then it stopped as if it couldn't go any further.

So the man decided to help the butterfly. He took a pair of scissors and snipped off the remaining bits of cocoon. The butterfly emerged easily, but it had a swollen body and shriveled wings.

The man continued to watch it, expecting that any minute the butterfly's wings would enlarge and expand enough to support its body. Neither happened! Instead, the butterfly spent the rest of its life crawling around, unable to realize its full potential. It was never able to fly.

What the man in his kindness and haste did not understand was this: the restrictive cocoon, and the struggle required by the butterfly to get through its tiny opening, was a way of forcing the fluid out from the body into the wings so that it would be ready for flight once it fully emerged.

Sometimes, struggles are exactly what we need in our lives in order for us to achieve our goals. Going through life with no obstacles is actually a crippling experience. Without struggling at some point, we can't hope to be as strong as we could be, because we're never able to comprehend what we're truly capable of.

Here is a simple yet profound exercise that will help you change your perspective with regard to challenges. Take some time to reflect on your life. From what circumstances have you learned the most? Have you faced challenges that initially seemed insurmountable, and if so, were you forced to grow spiritually and build your character in order to succeed? I'll bet the answer to that is yes! When things are going well, we tend to get comfortable. However, when faced with a challenge, we are forced to strive for another level in order to adjust, cope and overcome. You suddenly find resources and talents you had no idea you possessed and would never have known had things continued to go smoothly.

That's exactly the place I found myself in while waiting for Damien to wake up from his coma. For eight days, his mother, his sister and I sat beside his bed, alternately talking to Damien as if he were awake and praying to God to give him back to us. Hour after hour, we kept this up, and when the feelings of helplessness threatened to take me over, I asked the Lord for His will to be rendered and to help me accept Damien's fate, whatever that might be. I also asked Him to allow me to be a source of help to someone else, no matter what.

Each moment of those eight days seemed to last an eternity as we waited to see if his condition would improve.

Then one day, the doctors announced that Damien's healing had progressed to the point where they could attempt to bring him out of the coma. Encouraged by the news, we were nevertheless very anxious as we watched him gradually return to consciousness. What happened next was nothing short of a miracle: after just eight weeks of intense rehabilitation, Damien, aside from a few facial scars, had made a full recovery!

As any parent can attest, seeing your child hurt or sick is the worst kind of hell, and without my faith, I can honestly say I wouldn't have gotten through it. Now that I had climbed this tallest of "mountains", I not only sympathized, but empathized, with those who faced similar challenges every single day. Little did I know that it would ultimately help me while climbing Kilimanjaro. I learned that most of the challenges we face in life are not just meant for us, but for those who will need our help along the way.

Considering my experiences, I suppose it's fair to call me an optimist. I believe that when you are looking for something positive within a person or a situation, you will find it. Optimists try to seek the valuable lesson inherent in every setback. Rather than becoming upset and blaming someone else, optimists take control over their emotions and ask themselves, "What can I learn from this experience? Because I know, despite appearances, there has to be a lesson and a silver lining as well."

Every mountain has a valley, and every valley has a mountain. When you are climbing toward your goals, you will inevitably face valleys along the way. There will be temporary setbacks and even failures, but you must find a way to keep moving forward, no matter how difficult it may seem to do so. The trick is to not let your failures define you but to search for an alternate path. It may take a while, but if you persevere and don't let self-limiting thoughts eat away at you, you will eventually find something that works.

Fail Forward

Several years ago, after fifteen years of marriage and two children, I was facing divorce. It was devastating, and for four weeks or so I plummeted into one of the darkest, most painful places I have ever known. This experience tested my faith and my very will to move forward. I felt like a failure. Until that time, I'd always felt like I had known both the thrill of victory and the agony of defeat, but never had I faced such a treacherous peak as this, and never had I been so close to falling over the edge.

However, it is often during our darkest moments that we receive the teachers and the guidance that will lead us back to the light. For me, that teacher was a friend, and the guidance came in the form of a book, John C. Maxwell's *Failing Forward: Turning Mistakes into Stepping Stones for Success*, which he recommended. Reading this book gave me the energy I needed to refocus and brought me to the realization that *all* humans inevitably fail at times; it is one's outlook, perception, and response in the face of those failures that separates people who are defeated by failure and people who go on to achieve great success. I also learned that failure is not a single event but part of the process in the great journey we all undertake, and one's understanding of this impacts and characterizes every aspect of our lives.

Oftentimes, we are too quick to isolate events in our lives and label them as successes or failures instead of viewing them in the context of a bigger picture. We even go so far as to label other people as successes or failures and to internalize their criticisms of us. I've learned this is a sure-fire way to bring about more failure. The truth is, *I* am the only person who can label *my* actions as failure. *You* are the only person who can label *your* actions as failure.

Experiencing failure does not make you a failure—it makes you human! If your life is not going the way you want it to, it is time to examine your responses when things don't go your way. It will also be useful to look at how your *fear of failure* might be hindering your efforts. I have learned that people respond to the fear of failing as follows:

- Paralysis: They stop doing anything that might lead to failure.

- Procrastination: They develop a poor use of time and decline in productivity.

- Purposefulness: They avoid pain and the possibility of making mistakes, which also leads to inactivity.

Fear has been defined as "False Evidence Appearing Real." Each of us wants something, and each of us is afraid of something. We can't avoid feeling fear, but we can strive to conquer it. You have to be willing to feel the fear inside yourself, then take action in spite of it. You'll find that as soon as you take action, things become easier, and experience begets competence. The trick is to take that first step.

For me, that first step was realizing that inside every perceived failure is the opportunity to course correct and begin again. In the midst of a very painful divorce, I took full responsibility for what was happening and admitted my mistakes. To do this, I had to look beyond myself to the larger context of the relationship. It was a character-building exercise to say the least!

At the same time, I had to learn to neither project failure to the outside world nor let it become an inherent part of my being. No matter what happens to you, the process of coping with failure is an internal struggle. When faced with a seemingly insurmountable challenge or obstacle, ask yourself, "How do I want to be remembered with regard to my response to this situation? What story will be told of me?" Or, better yet, "When I look back on this situation, how do I want to remember my response? How did I use my failure as an opportunity for growth?"

My divorce, as painful as it was, turned out to be a pivotal moment for me. The law of human behavior states that, sooner or later, we get exactly what we expect, and I had to start expecting the best from myself and from my life. As I mentioned earlier, I am an optimist.

Psychologist and self-help author Martin Seligman has stated that people who bounce back are optimists. One can cultivate optimism by learning contentment. Contentment is not containment however. Containing your emotions will not lead to optimism and will not lead to the ability to recover from painful circumstances.

Contentment is not about money and power, nor is it about maintaining the status quo. It is about having a good attitude as you work yourself out of the rut you currently find yourself in. True contentment comes from seeing potential solutions in every problem and believing in oneself. It is the ability to hold onto hope no matter what happens to you.

Attitude determines Altitude. Challenges can only disable us if we let them. In the wake of our failures, the only real lasting limitations are those we create in our own minds.

I would carry these lessons with me as I prepared for my trip to Kilimanjaro. Based on my research and the advice of ClimbKili, the company I had hired to guide me up the mountain and for our Tanzanian adventures, I set the goals of my training program, taking into account the length, difficulty and challenges of my chosen route up Kili.

Six months prior to the climb, I, along with my gym and

climbing buddy John, began our fitness program. Our trainer encouraged us to be disciplined in improving cardiovascular and fitness training from the start, steadily increasing our regimen as we gained strength while being careful to avoid injuries. We paid extra attention to increasing our Vo2 maximum, the ability to raise our oxygen capacity. And, since we knew increasing lung capacity along with core and leg endurance would go a long way in preparing us for the climb into thinner air, we took long brisk walks in our hiking boots while carrying twenty-five-pound rucksacks on our backs. We focused on uphill and downhill training and navigated rocks, sand and hills, all in preparation for the changing terrain we could expect on the approach to Kilimanjaro. We even utilized the seven flights of stairs in our workplace.

Climbing the Mountain

Mountain climbing is viewed by some as an extreme sport, while for others it is simply an exhilarating adventure—a challenge of both physical and mental strength, endurance and sacrifice. It can be extremely dangerous and even fatal. When the climber is out of his or her depth, or simply gets overwhelmed by weather, terrain, snow, ice or other dangers on the mountain, disaster can result. Inexperience, poor planning and inadequate equipment can lead to injury or death, so knowing what to do in each potential situation is critical.

Despite the risks, when done right, mountain climbing

is an exciting and rewarding experience. It can also be, as it was in my case, an excellent teacher of life lessons. Indeed, successfully reaching the summit of Mount Kilimanjaro, the tallest free-standing mountain in the world, completely changed my perspective when facing obstacles, roadblocks and challenges—the "mountains" of life.

Turn One Day Into Day One

Someday never comes, and today was yesterday's tomorrow. Once you become clear about your goals, it's time to make an all-out commitment to realizing them.

Set timelines, and become guided by them. You've given yourself a roadmap to reaching your goal, so why not follow it? Remember to tell your close friends and family about your goals. They will keep you accountable and motivated so you will not lose face with them.

Frequently review your goals and measure your progress. If necessary, adjust your path, but keep your focus on the prize. Reaching the summit of your goals is a journey, so enjoy the hike. Celebrate every win along the way.

Day 1

After a seemingly endless flight, we were met at Kilimanjaro International Airport (JRO) by our climbing team representative and transported to our base hotel for a much-needed rest. The following morning, we had a detailed meeting with our head guide, who outlined the trek ahead. It would begin at the Londorossi Gate on the western side of Kilimanjaro—starting altitude, 7,742 feet.

I could see Kili in the far distance and was immediately filled with a mixture of excitement and fear. We had no sooner taken our first steps when the negative chatter going on in my head started to get the best of me. *Are you sure you want do this? Do you really want to put yourself in danger? What if you get sick? What about the wild animals? What about altitude sickness? You know you are asthmatic!* It literally felt like an avalanche of toxic thoughts tumbling down upon me. I began to hyperventilate and realized that for the first time in my life I was having a panic attack. My companions kept moving along with no idea that there was a war of emotions raging inside of me.

I stopped to retrieve my water bottle from my backpack and took slow sips as I tried to get my head together. Fortunately, I knew this would be a spiritual journey as well as a physical one and had prepared accordingly. "No weapon formed against me shall prosper," I told myself. "I can do all things through Christ who gives me strength; I am more than a conqueror through Him who loves me and gave Himself for me; He will keep me in perfect peace if I keep my mind focused on Him." And finally, "Wayne, see yourself standing on top of Kili!!"

The more I washed my mind with the positive, the more negative washed out! Moreover, I realized that with each *step, pole, pole,* the better I felt. Remember, while faith comes by hearing, faith without action is dead." And dead faith will keep you stagnated or moving backward.

When I got my thinking right, refocusing on my goal and acting as if I were already there, I began to enjoy the journey. Three miles and four hours later, on a trail that ascended and descended through a wondrous rainforest thick with trees and shrubbery, we arrived at Camp Mkubwa or "Big Tree" in Swahili. After signing the checkpoint register book, we high-fived each other in celebration of our successful day!

Day 2

After a night of being serenaded by a choir of all sorts of forest inhabitants, I was awakened by what sounded like a loud roaring train. It was actually a gang of black monkeys gathering high in trees over our campsite. I lay awake until our porter greeted us with tea and two basins of warm water. For the next eight days, it would be "soldier baths" and baby wipes. Then, after the briefing for that day's trek, we checked our list for backpack supplies, ate a breakfast of fruit, eggs, toast, sausage and oatmeal, then set off on the 4.5-mile, six-to-eight-hour trek at an altitude of 11,500 feet. As we left the rainforest, the air remained moist and thick with humidity, but the landscape changed dramatically from lush green foliage to a vast, nearly barren desert plateau. This was also the point at which Mt. Kilimanjaro came into majestic focus on the horizon, and I reminded myself while growing closer with every step.

Landmarks (Making Decisions)

"Every challenge you encounter in life is a fork in the road. You have the choice to choose which way to go—backward, forward, breakdown or breakthrough."

—Ifeanyi Enoch Onuoha

As we hiked, I absorbed every sight, sound and smell and tucked them into my memory. Up ahead, our guide, Saba, moved with easy confidence. Suddenly, it occurred to me that he did not have a visible map! I glanced from him to the porters[1] traveling with us and noticed that they also carried no maps.

---

[1]Porters were an indispensable part of the team. Every porter had his assigned responsibility: some assembled and unassembled the tents; others carried supplies and gear bags. Then there was "the forerunner"—he would leave each camp very early in the morning, make his way alone to the next camp and mark the site for us. I was quite in awe of them.

"You're walking along on this path, dazzled by how perfect it is, how great you feel, and then just a few forks in the road and you are lost in a place so bad you never could have imagined it."

—Huntley Fitzpatrick

After a while, our trail split off into three paths, each heading off in a separate direction. When I asked Saba how he knew which path to follow, he directed my attention to "rock formations." Made of rocks of various shapes and sizes, these formations had not been created by nature but by those who had used the trail before. They stacked the rocks in such a way so as to offer directions to those who were trained to read them. Treks were often washed out or became impassable due to heavy rains, Saba, the assistant to the head guide explained, so having another form of guidance was critical; it may even be a matter of life and death.

Listening to him, I realized that whether in climbing or in life, there are certain situations for which you will need a guide, and not just any guide, but one who is trained and experienced. Even with all the research I had done to prepare for this epic journey, I still needed help to guide me to the path that would get me to my destination.

To this day, the story of Saba and the rocks brings to mind one of my favorite Bible verses, Proverbs 3:6: "In all your ways acknowledge Him, and He will make your path straight."

But what do you do when you find yourself at a fork in the road and without an obvious guide like Saba? How do you choose the right direction?

I have come to such proverbial forks in the road many times in my life, circumstances that forced me to ask which route I should take. Through trial and error, I have learned important nuggets that not only gave me the keys to making wise decisions but ultimately put me on the path to my life's mission.

Below I share a few of those nuggets to assist you in finding the right path for your life:

1. Pray

Without exception, for me, prayer is the most powerful tool I have in life. All one has to say is, "Lord, I want what You want for me," then live in positive expectation and anticipation of his action on your behalf. But this is for you to discover for yourself whether that's true. Now, here comes the tricky part: resist the urge to run ahead of Him by trying to solve your problem yourself. Instead, be still and wait upon the Lord. Waiting can be difficult, I know! But He knows where all the emergencies are in your life, and He knows whether you are ready for the solutions. If you are not ready, and He gives it to you anyway, you might very well squander it. It is never that He is punishing you or doesn't want you to have something. It is simply that He knows the situations and/or people that need to change or be in place before He can answer your prayer.

When in the midst of painful or frustrating circumstances, we often say, "I know what I want; I can see it, so why should I ask Him and wait? Why would God listen to me anyway?"

Well with an attitude like that, He won't.

So, whether you understand it or not, PUSH (Pray Until Something Happens!) You might be asking, "What is going on during that time?" Maybe a lesson about trust and patience. He said, "Ask and it shall be given to you, but not right now."; "Seek and you shall find, but not today."; "Knock and the door shall be opened to you, but it might take a while." Rest assured, though, all His delays have purpose, and it's always for your highest good.

2. Look Out for Pressure

There are two types of pressure that can derail us and keep us from realizing our goals. The first is the external pressure we get from family, friends, colleagues, and society as a whole. Everyone has their own motives and perspectives, so when discussing, formulating and pursuing your goals, you must be very careful who you listen to. They may be well-meaning and tell you what you want to hear instead of what you need to hear; or, unfortunately, they may be jealous or have other reasons for discouraging you. Either way, you must use your discernment, and when you feel like your emotions are getting in the way, what I do is pray about it. For me, God is the only one who will never steer me wrong. This is a solution I use, and you're welcome to give it a try.

The other kind of pressure—internal pressure—can be even more dangerous because it is harder to detect. This is that voice in our heads that tell us we're not good enough or that our past failures determine our future. This type of negative self-talk can cause a whole host of problems, from choosing unrealistic goals and poor planning to procrastination and other forms of self-sabotage.

3. Stop Overanalyzing

Have you ever lay awake at night, unable to sleep for all the what-ifs and other thoughts racing through your mind? If so, you're not alone. At one time or another, we've all given the reins to stress and anxiety, especially in these days of the Internet and the twenty-four-hours news cycle. We are so bombarded with stimuli, it can be very difficult to turn our minds off. While it's great to have so much information at our fingertips, it gives us the illusion that we can know everything and perhaps even control it. The truth is most of our stress is rooted in overanalysis of everything from our relationships to business to how we can live a healthier lifestyle. Whatever our issues are, overthinking them is rarely productive.

No matter how advanced we think we are and how fast-paced the world is moving, we still cannot say with certainty where we will be in one year, five years, and so on. However, this is not necessarily a bad thing. Think about it—if where you end up in the future was limited to what you can conceive of today, you might be missing out on a plethora of gifts and opportunities that may be part of a much bigger plan for you. You would also have

no incentive to grow and see your life from a higher perspective. So stop obsessing about tomorrow and instead
make your choice based upon what's most important to
you today! When you come to understand and accept
that life is unpredictable, you can take a deep breath, stop
overanalyzing and start noticing what is being presented
to you in each moment.

4. Get a Move-on

Taking action always makes us feel better; it gives a sense
of purpose and power. Don't overanalyze or criticize; if
you take even one small step every day, you will soon find
yourself moving closer and closer to your goal. That said,
I believe there is one direction in which we are meant to
go and that is *forward*. This brings us back to the story of
the fork in the road and the rock formations. Any action
you take should be aligned with your goal and the road
map you've created to get there. When faced with a situation, obstacles, challenges, it is important to be able to
read and decipher the signs. Also, when deciding the best
action to take, don't forget to pray!

I continued to see evidence of these lessons while trekking
up and down the mountainous terrain that second day.
The trail was lined with rocks—which had been created
by ancient lava flow—mixed with other minerals. When
viewed through the ever-present mist and without the
assistance of the natural sunlight, these rocks appeared
quite ordinary—just grey, brown and black. However,

when illuminated by the sun, a host of beautiful copper, green and silver hues revealed themselves. Then there were the flowers of incredibly bold and vibrant colors; they flourished, seemingly against all odds, in this harsh, rugged terrain.

As I took in this incredible beauty, it struck me that we all possess hidden qualities that come to light only under the heat of trial. Consider a diamond, which forms under intense pressure, or a pearl, which starts as a spec of sand and an irritant to an oyster. There is beauty in all of us. We were made on purpose and for a purpose. Just like those lava rocks that glitter in the sunlight, when we allow "the Son" to shine through us, we become channels for His beauty. And just like the flora that blooms under the right conditions, we blossom when we allow Him to guide our footsteps to the right jobs, relationships, and situations.

Along with the changes in the landscape, that day brought a rather dramatic change in the weather. After lunch, as we started our final approach to SHIRA Campsite, we were ambushed without warning by wind and rain. The downpour was so forceful I could not see two feet in front of me, and we had to scamper under a nearby cliff so we could put on our rain gear. That's when I realized I had a problem: I could not find my raincoat, because I did not pack it! I stared down at my bag, unable to believe that despite going down my checklist before leaving camp, I had left out this very important item. Needless to say, I had to complete the remainder of the uphill trek bearing the full brunt of the cold, wind and rain. It was a true test of my stamina and willpower, and all I could do was keep going and pray that the rest of the trip would be flat. No such luck; after hiking for what felt like hours, we reached the top of a mountain only to see more hills and mountains as far as the eye could see. Our guides pointed out our campsite in the distance, and for a moment, my heart sank when I realized that to get there, we had a valley to traverse and another mountain to climb. Wet, cold and unsteady on my feet, I felt the doubt and questions like, **What were you thinking?** creep into my mind. It wasn't easy, but I forced myself to focus on my prayers and reminded myself that in climbing and in life, every mountain has a valley and every valley has a mountain. Quitting was not an option. The only answer was to keep moving forward.

Finally, we reached camp. The rain had stopped, and the clouds, which had obscured the majestic Kilimanjaro, had moved away. We signed into the checkpoint, and I headed quickly to my tent to get out of my wet clothes and drink some honey and ginger tea. While resting before dinner, John and I congratulated each other on a successful day's journey. Though somewhat restored by the tea, I was concerned about any effects the cold temperatures and wet clothes might have had on my health.

At dinner, I once again took in the beautiful scenery. Our campsite was nestled on a cliff between hills, overlooking a large, lush valley. As the evening progressed, I noted the temperature change again. I also felt the start of a nagging cough. After the meal, followed by a briefing about the next day's plan, I headed back to my tent for a much-needed rest.

Day 3

Early the next morning, we set out for the next leg of our journey—a 6.3-mile, six-to-eight-hour trek that would take us to Moir Camp at 13,800 feet, which is situated in a huge gorge at the end of a dormant lava flow. As we left our campsite behind, I kept my eyes on Kilimanjaro and wondered what this day would hold. Not wanting a repeat of the previous day, I was wearing my raincoat in case the weather turned again. However, it was too late to prevent the nagging cough I had developed, and that, coupled with an altitude of 11,500 feet, made it challenging to breathe. I pushed the worry to the back of my mind as I pressed forward, *walk, pole, pole,* to explore the Shira plateau. We were trekking eastward toward Kibo's glaciated peak where the ancient collapsed Shira cone, the oldest of Kilimanjaro's three volcanoes, could be seen.

Buried Alive

In the middle of the night, I was jolted from sleep by a coughing fit. As the hacking subsided, I heard what sounded like a train passing by and the tent being pelted with what I thought were rocks. It reminded me of a hurricane. This went on for what felt like forever. I feared that the tent would be blown away and us with it! I eventually drifted off out of sheer exhaustion only to be awoken again, this time by moisture dripping on my face. I reached for my flashlight and switched it on only to find myself face to face with my side of the tent roof. It had collapsed under the weight of what we later realize to be snow! Trying not to panic, I shifted the light to John's side and was a bit relieved to find it was not too bad. He had slept through the whole thing! I, on the other hand, lay there helplessly, praying that help would come before lack of oxygen became a problem. My thoughts ran to my family and other loved ones and the fear that I would never see them again. I could not call them on the phone or even text them! In those awful moments, I asked myself whether I had loved enough through my words and deeds, made the best of every opportunity, and what I would be remembered for. Was there anything I would do differently if given a second chance? Like the tent buckling under the weight and pressure of the snow, I felt myself starting to give up hope and giving into the real possibility of being buried alive. My cough was getting worse, my head felt as though it was going to explode with every cough, and my chest burned as if on fire. All of this was a lot less alarming, though, than the confined space and freezing temperature. I reached for my water bottle, but it had frozen solid! Condensation dripping above my head was just enough to wet my throat. I wrapped myself in my sleeping bag and prayed that help would come quickly!

I remember thinking, *Lord, I know You did not bring me all this way for my life to end like this. You are always in control and there is nothing too hard for You. Give me Your peace while I wait for Your deliverance.*

John eventually woke up, and after waiting for what felt like eternity, we heard, from out in the darkness, the muffled voices of our porters. The voices got louder and louder, asking if we were okay and telling us not to worry; they would get us out.

Have you ever felt like you're buried alive under life's challenges? Maybe you were drowning in debt, or suffocated by the loss of a love one through death or divorce, or overwhelmed by worry about the future. Maybe it's all of those things at once. If so, then you know that the worst part of having these problems is the feeling of utter helplessness that accompanies them. Perhaps you even needed to be rescued, as I did that morning. It was easy for me to accept help from the porters because I felt I was in immediate physical danger. It may be more difficult to accept assistance in daily life, from anyone, but when you've reached the point of overwhelm, it's time to set aside your pride. It may be a kind word, an inspiring idea or a favor—anything that allows you to see past your dark place and into the light of day!

The porters' voices gradually grew louder and clearer, then something miraculous happened: the darkness gave way to light! The tent had been so covered by snow that I did not realize morning had already arrived. Once the entrance to our tent was cleared, John and I crawled out to find that the landscape had completely changed from the night before. Amidst the shouts and hugs of relief and jubilation, I remember feeling a great sense of gratitude and rebirth.

I offer the story of the snowstorm as an example of how, no matter how well we think we've planned, we can be blindsided by life. Sometimes, these circumstances are so disorienting that we cannot see them clearly. That was what happened to me; I was lying there, praying for light, all the while completely unaware that it was just beyond view. The darkness was merely an illusion created by the snow, and it was only because of my faith that I had the strength, hope and peace to wait it out. Little did I know that this experience, while terrifying, had taught me a valuable lesson that I would call upon later in my journey.

When facing stormy conditions, most of us have asked, "Why me?" when in fact we should be asking, "What is the pearl of wisdom to be gleaned?" Though at some points I have certainly doubted the value of my challenges, I have learned that everything we face—the good, bad and ugly—is necessary for building our character and faith; they are part of the greater mosaic of our lives.

My favorite analogy for this is the jigsaw puzzle. You're searching for one particular piece and can't seem to find it. You look and look and even start telling yourself that the manufacturer left it out. Or you put the border together but cannot seem to find the right pieces to bring it all together. It is only when you surrender to the process that you are successful in completing the big picture. The same is true of our path in life. It is not always clear and detailed; we certainly don't have the picture on the puzzle box to go by! And, like the puzzle, the more pieces we have in life, the more intricate, complicated, and time-consuming it will be. I hold to the belief that the Lord is in every detail of my life and has perfect knowledge of me right down to the last detail. He knows where and how every piece, every experience, every challenge, every victory and every fall fits into the tapestry of my life! That is why it makes sense to trust Him, not only in the good times, but the bad as well. I have come to the realization that he loves us so much that He spared no expense so that we can live in abundance, and each and every mountain we face serves as preparation for what is to come. Think about it: there are challenges you face today that you know you can overcome and you know how to do it because you have done it before. It is my experience that the Lord does not lead me where He has not first prepared me for. Whenever He has ordered my footsteps, He has also provided everything and everyone I needed to complete the assignment or task. And when outward appearances have made me ask, "What in the world is going on?" faith has always shown me the wisdom to know what to do. Now let me be clear, the Lord *always* answers. It may not be what you or I want, but it is always what you need. And when the two line up, well, that we call miraculous!

If you're like me, this kind of trust is not automatic but hard-won after years of wrong turns born of impatience and ego. How many times have you convinced yourself that you had to have this or that, or him or her, and you had to have it/them *right now*? No matter how many times you encounter roadblocks or other signs telling you *no* or *not right now*, you push on, determined to have your own way on your own time. It is only later, when what you wanted was not all it was cracked up to be, that you realize you actually do not know it all. You see how much wasted time, money and heartache could have been avoided if only you had trusted and waited for His answer.

Sometimes, it takes a radical event to change one's per-spective. For me, it was nearly freezing to death in that partially collapsed tent in the snow. I was gifted with the opportunity to reflect on my life and the way I did things, and, as a result, I emerged into the cold, crisp air a changed man. I knew without a doubt that no matter what lay ahead of me, on Kili and in life, I was equipped to face it! I also knew that I had not equipped myself (remember, with all my planning, I had still forgotten my raincoat the day before. The Lord would never send me out in the storm without the proper protection).

The good news is, you don't need to come close to death in order to have such an epiphany. You can do it through your imagination. Try to visualize yourself buried in that tent. Outside, the wind is howling and the only light you have is from a weakening flashlight. If someone does not come soon, you could be buried alive. What would you think about? What would you wish you could have done differently? Who would you have treated differently? Then, suddenly, you are delivered from death and given a second chance. How would that experience affect you, your decision-making, and your entire outlook on life? Would you see the rescue as "pure luck" or a gift from God? Would it make you more thankful, more giving, more loving, more humble? Would it inspire you to look for and embrace opportunities to help others? Would you live your life with more of an open hand rather than a clenched fist?

Day 4

On today's agenda was an acclimatization trek to Lava Tower. Following our rest at the Tower, we would visit the enormous waterfalls of the Senecio forest before arriving at Barranco Camp. There, we would set up camp in the shadow of the massive Barranco Wall.

For the first time, we were joined by other climbers converging from several other routes for the trek up to Lava Tower, an important acclimatization point at 15,000 feet. The high altitude made climbing increasingly difficult, as did the wind and snow, which at times was knee-deep! Let's just say I was very grateful for my poles, which helped with traction, and the special eyewear that protected my eyes from the glare of the sun reflecting off the snow. After reaching Lava Tower, we stopped for lunch before a quick descent through a forest and rocky terrain. To say this was different from our ascending snow-covered trek would be an understatement! At times, we were actually running down the slopes through waterfalls and rivers created by the snow melting high on the mountain. The lower we got, the higher the temperature, and we found ourselves stripping off layers of clothing to help us acclimate to the lower altitude. Finally, we reached our camp, which was beautifully perched on a rocky plateau on the side of a mountain, high above the Barranco Valley. The view would have to wait a bit, however; with every muscle in my legs and back throbbing, I settled in for a much-needed rest before dinner. Tonight's menu was vegetable soup, pasta and lots of milo or honey ginger tea.

Day 5
Hitting a Wall

After a rainy night, we exited our tent to find that the landscape had once again been reconfigured. The torrential downpour had washed away several tents belonging to climbers in the lower lying areas, and though thankfully no lives were lost, much of their gear, food and supplies were. Sadly, for some, this meant the end of their quest to reach the summit of Kilimanjaro.

Our dining tent was also a casualty of the storm, but we otherwise seemed to be unscathed. It wasn't until upon further inspection of our tent that John and I noticed that the rain storm had washed rocks and boulders off of the surrounding high areas down to where we had set up camp. Several large rocks had come to rest just outside our tent, right in the spot where our heads were! We stood there, our bewilderment turning to gratitude when we realized what we had been saved from!

After a baby wipe bath and breakfast, it was time to climb Barranco Wall. This was an incredible mental and physical challenge, especially for those with a problem with heights. We had to scramble straight up the six-hundred-foot wall using only our hands and feet as there was not enough room for poles. What a workout! I remember thanking God that I had done all those pull-ups during training. When we reached the top, our hard work was rewarded with a view even more spectacular than I had imagined. We were literally above the clouds! Our mood matched the altitude, with everyone high-fiving each other for conquering the mighty Barranco Wall! What a feeling of gratefulness and accomplishment.

On the climb up Kilimanjaro, the Barranco Wall is a significant milestone—a point of no return that solidifies one's commitment to Kili itself. For me, and I suspect many other climbers, it is also a spiritual milestone as well, a barrier standing between the past and the future. To cross that barrier, one must push themselves past the limits of human endurance; there is no respite, only straight up! I am told that marathon runners, when they reach the five, ten or twenty-mile mark, often get tired and weary and want to give up. They call this "hitting the wall," and if they want to finish, they must find a way to push past it and keep going. I asked two accomplished runners what they do when faced with their personal wall. They told me that they rely on their training and past experience to push past what their body is telling them. In other words, they get their mind to control the body. They use the memory of their past achievements to propel themselves forward, and before they know it, they are pushing past the wall that had seemed insurmountable.

Even if you never climb Kili or run a marathon, you too will face your own Barranco Wall; in fact, you will probably face several. Here are some strategies to help you scale them:

- Remind yourself of past struggles and how you overcame them to achieve your goal.

Until that morning, I had never faced a physical mountain or wall like that. But I had in the recent past faced other challenges that gave me the fortitude I needed to say, "I can do this!" and mean it. This, along with encouragement and inspiration from others, helped get me to the top.

The next time you're about to say you can't do something, stop and ask yourself, "What lessons have I learned from past experiences that I can hold onto now to get me over this wall?"

- Speak to a mentor and/or others who empower you. Avoid those who drain your strength.

We all need positive people in our lives—those who will act as our cheerleaders and push us onward and upward. Seeing the other climbers put their best foot forward and encouraging each other took me out of my own head. It reminded me that though we were individuals, we shared a common goal. This got my adrenalin pumping so I could keep going and act as a source of encouragement for the others. When you empower others, you empower yourself. Remember, "No man is an island," and sooner or later we are going to need help from someone else. I encourage you to find someone to honor, put their concerns before yours and watch the positive impact it has on both of you.

- Remind yourself that failure is not an option (i.e. "No matter what it takes, I am going to do this.")

When I was a child, everything I needed was handed to me—food, clothes, love. I wanted for nothing. My parents protected me from harm whenever possible and made sure I had whatever tools I required to get over "the wall."

And whenever I complained that things weren't going my way, they would remind me that I did not know how good I had it! As an adult, there have been times when I expected life to treat me as my parents did. That's when I had to remind myself that I have all the tools I need to face my walls. I just have to tell myself, "You can do this."

That said, we also must be vigilant about what we allow into our lives. What/who we watch and listen to has great control over us, so it's a good idea to regularly check in and ask, "What am I feeding myself?" If I am constantly telling myself *I can't*, guess what? I won't! Equally so, if I tell myself that *I can*, then more often than not, I will!

After a short break, we made our way to Karanga Camp. Mountains and valleys as far as the eye could see! As we went down then slowly *pole, poled* up again, often in a zigzag motion, it hit me once again that climbing mountains was just like tackling life; you're either heading up toward a peak or descending into a valley.

I recall that after a steep descent to a valley floor, we were immediately faced with a long, steep incline. We were in our usual formation, with one guide leading the way up the winding path, then myself, followed by John. Another guide brought up the rear. The lead guide set the pace.

We had been slowly making our way up in a zigzag fashion (which allowed us to acclimatize to the higher altitude) when I had the bright idea to take a shortcut. Instead of following the guide, I veered off and took a straighter path and sure enough made it to the top in good time. I was also gasping for breath and sat down on a rock, which is where the others found me a while later. The guide was furious.

"Do not do that again!" he snapped. "My job is to get you to the top of Kilimanjaro and back to base camp safely. A shortcut can be the long way and a quicker way to altitude sickness and off the mountain."

I looked up at him, my initial shock turning to the realization that he was right. In my haste to get to the top, and my desire to prove that I knew better than the guide, I had been sabotaging myself! Fortunately, the only price I paid for my foolishness was a worsening of my nagging cough.

As I sat there on a large lava rock in my embarrassment, I reflected on my actions and asked myself how many times I had taken a shortcut in my life rather than waiting and allowing the Lord to lead me. How many times had I run ahead thinking I knew the way only to make matters worse or had gotten lost altogether? I further reflected on the fact that it is one thing for me to be affected by my actions, but it is a great difference when my actions affect others. Talk about self discovery!

Day 6

When I awoke the next morning, I decided to put the previous day's folly behind me and focus on the next leg of the journey. Today, we would be starting at an altitude of 13,106 feet and embarking on a 3.4-mile, four-to-five-hour trek to Barafu Camp at an elevation of 15,331 feet. It was a magnificent route, giving us excellent views of the Kibo and Mawenzi peaks. Barufu itself is situated on an exposed ridge, providing majestic sunsets. There, we would acclimatize and make necessary preparation for the summit day ahead.

Kissing the Clouds

This was a long and grueling trek in cold, snow-blown conditions. We trudged through a long canyon with visibility at times reduced to two or three feet in front of us. Everyone struggled to the point that our guides sometimes slowed the pace almost to a shuffle. At every rest stop, we sat drinking our ginger tea and honey while checking our vitals and encouraging each other. It was the team that kept me going when my cough, exacerbated by the dry, cold, increasingly thinning air, made it very difficult to keep putting one foot in front of the other. There were even times when I thought about ending my quest, but my compatriots' encouraging words and my own inner compass reminded me that quitting was not an option.

After reaching base camp, which was perched on a cliff face at the base of Kili, we placed chairs in the sunlight to rest and rejuvenate before dinner. There were over a hundred climbers there, which made it very busy and crowded. Every muscle in my body ached, and my feet and face were very cold. While sipping on my ginger tea, I was reflecting on the day's events when suddenly clouds blocked out the sun, plunging us into complete darkness. Screams and shouts filled the air, shaking me to my core. Then, as quickly as the darkness fell, the sun emerged again, almost seeming brighter than before. This happened several times, and, each time, it became less unnerving.

As the fear subsided, I realized that clouds, though dark, were very rejuvenating as they passed over my face. What a feeling! They made me forget my sore muscles and exhaustion. It was then that I understood that not every dark experience is a scary one. The next time the darkness descended, I decided to embrace the moment and "kiss the clouds." This was both invigorating and sobering. When faced with dark moments, you may feel as though you will never see the light of day again. But if you only stop and look for the clouds to refresh you, reflect on your best moments, and look for the "silver lining," you'll find that they will eventually blow away to reveal the sun. And, always, when waiting seems too hard, turn to your faith and remind yourself that "this too shall pass."

Day 7

We started off at midnight: the thirteen-mile, twelve-to fourteen-hour trek to an altitude of 19,340 feet to conquer the highest point in Africa. This section of the route is considered one of the steepest of the non-technical paths of Kilimanjaro. The first leg of this route, which would take six or seven hours, would get us to Stella Point in time to see the sunrise. From Stella Point, it would be an hour to Uhuru Peak and the rooftop of Africa. We would then descend to reach Mweka Camp by evening.

Stella Point

After dinner, our two guides gave us the final plan of action, what to wear and what to pack in our backpacks, and a medical assessment. The severe cough I had developed on Day 2 gave the team concerns. To be very honest, I was also concerned, but I told them that I had come here not just to see the base of Kilimanjaro but to view it from the top, and no cough was going to stop me. When I passed the H.A.S. (high altitude sickness) test, the head guide agreed to allow me to climb. He then instructed the chef to prepare more honey ginger tea for the climb. We went back to tent to gather our things. There weren't a lot of clothes to pack, as we slept in everything except our weather jackets and boots, but I did place my inhaler and energy bars in my bag. The water bottles would be filled just before leaving camp. After writing in my journal, I tucked a paper with the names of loved ones in my jacket, a symbol that this journey was one for all and all for one.

I then lay down, trying to get some rest before we set out, but between the cough and the thoughts racing through my mind, I found it difficult to sleep. I even tried to sleep sitting up! Finally, at 11:30 p.m., I emerged from the tent and joined the scores of others waiting to start our ascent. As we left the camp area, we were encouraged by the well wishes of the porters who stayed behind.

Just a few minutes of hiking under the full moon, we were met with an unwelcome surprise: snow. We expected to encounter snow on top of the mountain but not on the way up! Even the guides were shocked. This made an already challenging trek all the more difficult, even treacherous.

As the path became slushy and slippery, I lost my footing so often it felt as though I was climbing the mountain twice. Sometimes, our guide had to find new paths, which presented another problem as we needed to zigzag in order to acclimate and decrease the risk of high altitude sickness. Chanting the words, "Pole pole, slow slow," we soldiered on. It was very cold at the start, and it would only get colder the closer we got to the top.

About an hour in, my cough was making it difficult to breathe, and my inhaler did not work. It was through sheer force of will that I pushed myself forward. Looking back, I don't know quite how I did it, though I remember that the encouragement from John and our guides, as well as seeing the other climbers ahead, was a great help. Though I had faced many challenges in my life, I had never had to dig deep like this. With every step, I reminded myself that it was either sink or swim. Turn back, or keep going onward and upward.

This leg of the journey in particular taught me much about my mental toughness. I found myself questioning God and at the same time reminding Him of the agreement (about my reaching the top of Kili) we'd made when I was back in Bermuda. In the meantime, quitting was becoming more tempting, and more acceptable, as we would periodically come across someone who had decided they would not continue, or could not, due to altitude sickness or some other ailment. When this happened, I turned my thoughts to those of us determined to stay the course. I remember thinking how happy I was that it was still dark and I could not see the distance to the top. If I had, I too might have given up.

There will be times on your journey when you will not be able to see the finish line; you may not even be able to see the path in front of you. And, believe it or not, there will be times when the darkness is actually your friend, allowing you to step out into the unknown without seeing too much too soon. When this happens, recognize it as an opportunity to walk in faith. All too often, we refuse to take action unless we can see every step of the way for fear that some awful fate awaits us in the darkness. However, when we commit our way to the Lord and trust, He will guide us to the right paths. Playing safe is anything but safe. Sure, we may avoid some harrowing twists and turns, but we will also miss opportunities, leave mountains unconquered, relationships ruined or never started at all, and our full potential and purposes unfulfilled.

By daybreak, I knew I had to have a serious conversation with myself. I was exhausted mentally and physically. If not for the very real nagging cough and numbness in my feet, I might have thought I was dreaming the whole thing. Stella Point was visible, but it was still an hour's hike away. The way I felt, it might as well have been a day away. At that moment, I was prepared to forfeit the summit and settle for Stella Point (*almost* there!)

First, I reminded myself that though I was not yet where I wanted to be, I was also not where I started out. Many people never made it to this point! I reminded myself that while Stella Point was not my ultimate goal, it was a significant milestone on the road map to my goal. Stella Point was within reach, and from Stella Point, I knew the summit of Kili was visible. It was within reach as well.

Sometimes, the enormity of our goal can be so over-whelming that we're tempted to give up. Even if success is in sight, we feel it is out of reach. That's when we need to look back on how far we've come and how many interme-diate goals we've already reached.

Now, sometimes, that is the end of that particular journey. Like the rains that swept away the other hikers' tents and sent them home, there can sometimes be circumstances outside our control, hints that God is saying, "Not now." In those situations, we need to celebrate and be grateful for what we've already achieved and trust that God will present the opportunity again.

Then there are the times when you're just sick and tired of the challenges and are tempted to take the easy way out; you are tempted to settle for your Stella Point. This was the choice I was faced with on the trail that morning. Do I quit once we reach Stella Point, or do I continue to the summit?

When I told my team that I could go no further, they reminded me what we had agreed to several days earlier at the hotel.

"Kama smaki mu maji," our head guide had said. Roughly translated, this means, "We are like fish in water." It is the Swahili way of saying, "We are in this together."

So with one teammate on my right, another on my left, and John urging me on, they pulled me step by step, pole by pole, to Stella Point.

When we got there, I told the rest of the team to leave me and continue on to Uhura Peak. By the time they would return, I would be ready to trek down the mountain. But they refused to leave me, first, because they did not want me to go to sleep and, second, because of our agreement to stick together.

"See the peak?" they said. "That's what you trained for. That's what you prepared for. That's why you came all this way. That's why you endured the snowstorm."

Even my frozen feet couldn't argue with that one! So after a health check and a cup of ginger tea (our water was frozen solid), I summoned every ounce of my will and accepted their help. Once again assisted with guides on my left and right, I told myself with every step, "Yes I can!!" I began to recite my favorite bible verses ("I can do all things through Christ who strengthens me") and focused on my children, family and friends, and the charity[2] that was to benefit from my reaching the summit. With a renewed mind and determination, I watched in awe as the darkness that had shrouded my destination now gave way to bright sunshine and a clear view of the snow-covered path before us.

---

[2] I am the Chairman of Prison Fellowship Bermuda. Before leaving on my quest, I crafted pledge sheets for those willing to donate for every campsite I reached and, ultimately, reaching the top of Kili. This was a way for me to support a worthy charity that does great work in our community.

A couple of years after my climb, I came across a story that reminded me of those last hours struggling toward the summit. On January 15, 2015, Hyvon Ngetich of Kenya was leading the elite women at the twenty-third mile marker of the Austin Marathon when she suddenly collapsed. Medical personnel rushed toward her with a wheelchair, but Ngetich refused it and instead crawled the last fifty meters on her hands and knees until she crossed the finish line.

Race Director John Conley said of Ngetich's display, "You ran the bravest race and crawled the bravest crawl I have ever seen in my life." Conley adjusted Ngetich's purse prize to reflect second place.

When asked why she did not give up and why she had refused help, she replied, "You have to keep going. You have to keep Running! You need to die Running!"

Day 8
Building a Good Support Team

As my Stella Point story illustrates, a strong support system of coaches, mentors and friends is not only important, but vital. They can figuratively—or in my case, literally—be the stability needed to get you to the finish line. As we slowly made our way to Uhuru, they kept telling me how great it would be when we got there. They spoke positively to my negative outlook. Like water to a thirsty man, encouraging words refresh and revive a weary spirit! The more they encouraged me, the more I believed I could! Though I was still exhausted, every step got easier. My attitude was clearly shaping my altitude. I realized when I looked back over my life that God had always placed exactly the right persons in my life at exactly the right time.

Take a moment to consider the people currently in your life. Do they help or hurt? Do they build you up or tear you down? Do they know you and your values well enough to tell you the truth and hold you accountable for your action or inaction?

On the flip side, what kind of person are you in relation to them? What do you expect of them? What are you willing to be and do for them? These are the difficult questions we rarely ask ourselves, partly because the answers could upend our lives. However, they could also be incredibly healing and positive. Sometimes, they can even set us on a new, exciting course.

We are made to be social beings. As it states in Ecclesiastes 4:9-12, "Two are better than one, because they can help each other to succeed. If either of them falls down, one can help the other up. But pity anyone who falls and has no one to help them up. Also if two lie down together, they will keep warm. But how can one keep warm alone?"

If you have not figured it out yet, at one point or another, we are all going to need someone to help us in some way. We too will also be called upon to help someone else. This reciprocity is what our relationships, families and communities—our very world—are based on.

As we made our way up the snow-covered mountain, we passed those who had succumbed to exhaustion and high altitude sickness and were receiving medical attention. They had gone as far as they could and would now have to be evacuated off the mountain.

Those of us still pressing upward were encouraged by their shouts of "Jammbo[3], make it for me!" Their voices were like a beacon in the darkness, calling me toward my goal.

Heading into the unknown was scary and uncomfortable! As I fought my cough, fatigue and bone-chilling cold, all I had was my gut conviction that I would soon be standing atop Kilimanjaro.

As the peak drew closer, I found myself overwhelmed again, this time not by exhaustion but by emotion. I stopped to marvel at the majestic glaciers. Walls as high as three or four-story buildings came into view. Words failed me, and as my guide encouraged me to keep moving toward the peak, which was now just yards away, all I could say was, "Wow."

As we inched closer, we were met by those who had already reached Uhura Peak and were now making the two-hour trek back down to base camp. They greeted us with smiles and high fives, which we heartily returned. Then, suddenly, there it was: the sign congratulating us for reaching Uhuru Peak summit, 5,895m (19,340 feet). The team came together in celebration as I breathed a prayer of thanksgiving and praise. After taking photos to document this achievement, I reached into my inner coat, removed the paper containing the names of family and

---

[3]A Swahili salutation, similar to hello.

loved ones and placed it under a rock at the base of the sign. *All for one,* I thought, *and one for all!*

I had made it. I had reached the rooftop of Africa and one of my life's most challenging goals!

As we stood there, taking in the panoramic view, I was struck with the enormity of what we had done. It was as if my muscles knew it too; the adrenalin was pumping, and all feelings of exhaustion had evaporated. Now, as I reflect on all the obstacles, challenges, all the planning, preparation, training, financial and physical sacrifices, the idea of each of us having our own personal mountains to climb came into view. Through faith in God, determined action, and a mindset of "I can do this," I used those challenges to propel to the heights upon which I now stood. At the end of the day, they had not hindered me—though it often appeared so in the moment—but had pushed me forward.

Anyone, regardless of where they come from, can cultivate an unstoppable attitude! We will all have challenges in life; we will all be knocked down, and this attitude is necessary in order to reach our summit. An unstoppable attitude is that voice whispering, *I will not quit; I will not settle for "almost there"; I will get back up one more time than I have fallen. I will seize every opportunity to keep putting one foot in front of the other. I will invest the time and any financial, physical and spiritual resources at my disposal in order to get where I want to be.*

I will develop and cultivate the right relationships and value the gift of life. I will live intentionally, passionately and on purpose. I will, before acting rashly, stop and ask for direction with the understanding that every piece fits and all is connected.

That day on the summit, I was standing not only on a combination of lava rock, ice and snow but on all my past experiences, each of which had served as physical and spiritual stepping stones. Indeed, "all things work together for my good."

This new perspective filled my body and soul as we descended the mountain. That day, a new mantra was formed as well—"I climbed Kili, I can do this!" It rang through my mind with every step and fall of my now steady feet.

Poet and essayist Kathleen Norris wrote, "Before you begin a thing, remind yourself that difficulties and delays quite impossible to foresee are ahead. You can only see one thing clearly and that is your goal. Form a mental vision of that and cling to it through thick and thin."

A mantra, which is defined as "a sure and defined statement that inspires and motivates," can be critical in helping form our goals and keeping them in focus.

Realization is the Key

I want to inspire you to settle on your own mantra. When you are weary and fatigued with whatever you are facing, your mantra will be the inspiration and motivation to push you forward, even when you feel like you have nothing left to give. It will help when the negative chatter comes from within and from without. There are and will be those times when no one will be around to encourage you, so you need to encourage yourself!

We are often told, "You need to do this or that," but what about the how? (That's the part most people forget about.) The key to the "how" is **Don't sabotage yourself.**

Don't remind yourself of past failures but of your successes. Your past cannot hold your future hostage unless you allow it to.

Negative people say, "Remember what happened the last time...?"

Positive people say, "I already accomplished (insert a previous achievement), so I know I can do this!"

When creating your mantra or affirmation, you want to:

1. Keep it simple. Mantras do not need to be long. Come up with a sentence or phrase of just a few words.

2. Speak and use positive words in the present tense, i.e., "I am ... I can ... I know ... Avoid words like **not, have to** and **should.** Focus on the end result you want to achieve.

3. Feel and experience what you are saying rather than simply reciting words and phrases.

In order to be effective, a mantra must include these ingredients.

This practice also requires consistency. Repeat your mantra until you no longer give it a thought because it is a part of you. It will take time for your mantra to affect and change your mindset, so patience is a must.

To create your mantra, start by writing down your proudest achievements or successes. It does not matter how big or small these achievements are; it is not about judging them but about your feelings when you think of them.

This brings me to the next step. As you look over your list, take note of how each accomplishment makes you feel, then select the one that makes you feel the strongest and most confident. Do your best to reduce feelings to a word or short phrase. That's it! Now you have a statement of the greatness inside you. Use it consistently in good times and in challenging times. It will remind you how much you have grown and what you are capable of; it also speaks to your character and will give you the confidence to climb any mountain.

There are also more general mantras that will give you that added inspiration, such as: "Go for It!"; "I am special!"; "I believe!"; "I got this!"; "Celebrate life!"; "Blessed!"; "Live in the moment!"; "Gratitude!"; "Grateful!" "Live, laugh, love!"; and "Mind over matter!"

Don't you just feel your mood lifting as you read them? All of these mantras will serve as motivation when you are facing the "impossible"!

The Journey is Ongoing

I thought it would be easier getting off the mountain

than climbing up. Boy, was I wrong! There were two or three feet of snow on the ground, and that, coupled with gravity, made it very difficult. It seemed we spent more time rolling and tumbling down the mountain face than walking. Yet, somehow it did not matter, for I still had our triumph at the forefront of my mind. As we approached camp, I thought I heard singing. Was it my imagination? A hallucination born of exhaustion and hunger? It was neither. When we reached our campsite, we were greeted by our porters who were singing a song of celebration. When I asked our guide why they were so excited, he replied, "Because you succeeded, they too feel that they have succeeded. Remember, we are like fish in water, we all are in it together!"

After getting into dry clothes and resting, I thought about what I had just experienced, how grateful I felt for being celebrated! Though I was tired, aching all over, and had bruised toes on both feet, I was alive and grateful to be able to tell the story. After a much-welcomed hot meal, we started our final hour-and-a-half descent to the base check-in station to end our expedition.

This following Swahili song of celebration was sung by my guides and porters after a successful trek. It's a lively and happy song meant to be sung in rejoicing voices, often while dancing and clapping.

Jambo! Jambo bwana!

Habari gani? Mzuri sana!

Wageni, mwakaribishwa!

Kilimanjaro? Hakuna matata!

Tembea pole pole. Hakuna matata!

Utafika salama. Hakuna matata!

Kunywa maji mengi. Hakuna matata!

Kilimanjaro, Kilimanjaro

Kilimanjaro, mlima mrefu sana.

Na Mawenzi, na Mawenzi

Na Mawenzi, milma mrefu sana

Ewe nyoka, ewe nyoka!

Ewe nyoka, mbona wanizunguka

Wanizunguka, wanizungka

Wanizunguka wataka kunila nyama

Here is the English version:

Hello! Hello sir!

How are you? Very well!

Guest you are welcome!

Kilimanjaro? No trouble!

Walk slowly, slowly. No trouble!

You'll get there safe. No trouble!

Drink plenty of water. No trouble!

Kilimanjaro! Kilimanjaro!

Kilimanjaro, such a high mountain.

Also Mawenzi, also Mawenzi!

Also Mawenzi such a high mountain.

Like a snake, like a snake!

Like a snake you wrap around me.

You wrap around me, you wrap around me

Trying to eat me like a piece of meat.

Conclusion

It has been exciting to walk you through my personal "mountain to climb" experience. My deepest wish is that it will help you discover and rediscover the principles needed to help you reach your own summit.

Shortly after arriving safely back home, I realized that I saw life from a distinctly higher vantage point. I am very aware that I was a very different man from the one who had set off to climb Kili, and I promise that you will also be transformed every time you reach the summit of your goals. You will be more experienced and inspired, not only to face life but to succeed in whatever you put your mind to. You have extraordinary opportunities before you, possibilities limited only by your ability to dream and believe that it's possible! Go ahead and expose yourself and tell your story, just as I have done in the pages of this book.

Believe it or not, writing this book turned out to be another "Kili", for me, albeit a less physically harrowing one. Having never written a book before, I quickly realized how challenging it was! To keep me on track, I followed the recipe like an executive chef, tasting as he goes to produce the desired results. Along the way, I was blessed to meet several people in search of the tools to reach their goals. In short, they needed the advice I was providing! This encouraged and inspired me to keep going, even when the process became frustrating.

I have learned that there will never be the perfect time to start pursuing your dreams. I also learned that there is just one thing that separates successful people from the "wannabes." Successful people take action regardless of fear, challenges or opposition. They don't worry that they can't fly. They just jump and grow their wings on the way down.

Right now, you may be saying, "This sounds great, but where do I start?" Here is a mini roadmap designed to get you going:

Envision: What is your Kili? There is a Kilimanjaro in all of us, which we must overcome in order to live our full potential! Choose something you want to achieve. Write it down and in detail. By doing this, you will have a better visualization of what it is you wish to accomplish. It will also give hope in times of disappointment and despair. It will motivate you during times of discouragement. When you have a clearer vision of your goal, you will have a realization of that goal.

Condition your thinking by creating your own vision board for this project and reviewing it daily. Achieve your next goal, whether climbing a hill or a mountain, small or large, by proper planning and research. Obviously, this will be commensurate to the size of your goal. The following questions will help to identify and clarify your personal goals:

- What is my number-one goal?

- What consumes my thinking?

- What would I do if I knew that I could not fail?

- What would bring me fulfillment and a sense of purpose?

- What information do I need, and where can I find it?

- Who should I consult?

- What is the cost?

- Do I need to educate myself?

- What do I have to work with?

"Plans fail for lack of counsel, but with many advisers they succeed."

—Proverbs 15:22

Once you have vision of your goal, you now can create a plan. This should be in detail. You can set smaller goals within your plan to keep you on target. This is helpful if your goal is a lengthy one like traveling to Africa and climbing Kilimanjaro, which had a lot of logistics involved and required other people.

Planning and Goal-Setting Check Sheet

Year:

Name:

List Three Spiritual Goals

List Three Family Goals

List Three Relationship Goals

List Three Health Goals

List Three Career Goals

List Three Financial Goals

Some Goal Ideas:

- Lose weight

- Spend more quality time with family

- Devote more time and attention to reading spiritual content

- Get out of financial debt

- Open an investment account

- Invest in myself through educational courses

- Make a major purchase

Once your plan is in place, you can begin preparations. This is equally important because you don't want to not reach your goal because you skimped on preparation. Can you imagine planning to run a marathon but putting no effort into training? Many with this philosophy have started the race, but few have finished, and those who managed did so with much pain and discomfort. Your plan will give you a checklist of things to execute.

Now take action! You have your goal visualized, planned, and you are prepared. For you to realize your goal and reach the summit of your goal, you must act today! Whatever obstacles you face, respond to them by moving forward—step, step, pole, pole!

Remember, *"What matters is not the size of the mountain but the strength of the mountain mover."*

—Author unknown

Remove All Limitations

"They turned back and tempted God, and limited the Holy One of Israel."

—Psalms 78:41

We serve a God of increase! He wants to do new things in our lives. We should always be rising to new levels, but I found that it is so easy to get stuck in a rut and just settle for the status quo. Sometimes, we think, *Well, I've reached my limits. I've gone as far as I can go. This is as happy as I'll ever be.* But if we're going to continue to increase and really experience God's best, we have to get our thinking lined up with His.

Let's back up a minute to the passage from Psalms above, in which the people limited the Holy One of Israel. I used to ask myself, *How can the all-powerful God, the Creator of the universe, be limited?* Then I realized, by our thinking! He can be limited in our lives by what we believe. Many people don't realize that it's their own wrong thinking that's keeping them from succeeding and keeping them in mediocrity.

Start now—take the limits off by choosing to believe God. Feed your faith by reading His Word. As you meditate on His promises with an open heart, you will see Him move greatly in your life, and you will experience the abundance He has prepared for you!

The closer you get to the top (your intended goal), the more treacherous it becomes. When climbing Kili, I encountered increasingly higher altitudes, thinning air and narrow paths covered in snow. Some of these bordered deep ravines—one misstep or slip and I would have become a casualty. In order to keep going, I had to focus not on the impossibilities but on what was possible!

Remember, yesterday's experience will help you face today's challenges, so stand in your greatness!!

Compete Only Against Yourself

One day, while participating in a for-fun bowling tournament, I found myself opposite the honoree/host—a beautiful, eighty-year-old lady who bowled very slowly but very effectively. At the start, I made up my mind that I was not about to let her beat me, but I ended up bowling my worst and lowest game of the tournament. The more I focused on her getting a strike or spare, all the while smiling, I might add, the worse I bowled. After she was declared the winner, she walked over, and, with a smile on her face, a twinkle in her eye and a hand on my shoulder, she said, "You lost and did not bowl to your full potential because you focused and bowled against me and not the lane."

Comparison is the thief of all joy. Stop comparing yourself to everyone else. Stand in your greatness! You are the best you!

And, finally: be patient!

A bamboo tree takes five years before it breaks the surface of the ground, but once it does, it can grow ninety feet in six weeks! If you are like me, there are those times when I am doing what I need to do, yet it seems as though nothing or very little is happening. I neither feel nor see any signs of progress.

But when I just stay with it and consistently water and nurture my dreams and goals, no matter what, then sooner or later I know I will see evidence of my hard work sprouting through the soil of faith. The same is true for you, my friends. See you at the peak!

About the Author

Ordained minister and certified life coach Dr. R. Wayne Swan holds a Ph.D. in Leadership Studies and is the founder of Crossroads Ministries, an organization dedicated to supporting men in their spiritual and social growth and development. He is also the Chairman of Prison Fellowship Bermuda, an outreach program designed for inmates and their families to assist with their restoration to society and journey of redemption.

Service to others is the central focus of his life and work, and what began as a personal challenge to climb Mount Kilimanjaro became an opportunity to share a message of courage, hope and faith in *The Mountain We Climb*. With nearly 20 years' experience as a minister and motivational speaker, Dr. Swan is adept at addressing the issues that matter and inspiring people to overcome their struggles.

Dr. Swan has traveled extensively throughout the world working in collaboration with churches and community organizations. Born, raised and residing in Bermuda, he is married with two adult children.